Good Morning Prayers

I0165036

Ann Reynolds

Publisher/Editor: Hopeand, Inc.(h.tdemp.org) / Dempsey
Graphics (dg.tdemp.org)

Bible Acknowledgments:

Scripture quotations are taken from the King James
Version Bible;

On November 4, 2010, I received a phone call that catapulted me into the Spiritual Warfare battle and trial of a lifetime.

You see, I have been serving God in my spare time since 1981 by using my gift of singing Gospel Music at Churches and events in the community and surrounding areas. Many have called me an Evangelist because of the anointing and calling on my life to lift up the name of Jesus and praise God while ministering in song to encourage others. Yet my service did not exempt me from the phone call that informed me that my youngest son, Damien, who was 35 years old, healthy, fit and in the prime of his life, was suffering a Major Hemorrhagic Stroke. (a stroke with a bleed on the brain). Surely this had to be a nightmare, but as fate would have it, I was wide awake. I immediately began to pray and God clearly revealed to me that this attack upon my son's body was not unto death. God's mighty hand took me into the Spirit where my son and I remain even to this day, safe in his arms. I hopped a flight to Atlanta and spent the next month flying back and forth to the Atlanta Hospital where Damien was in a medical coma in ICU for 18 days. After he recovered from life support, he was then transferred from ICU to another hospital through December. I also spent time with his fiance, Nicki, her 4 year old son, Kaden and their 6 month old daughter, Taylor, as we both worked diligently to handle Damien's medical affairs. We did a lot of praying and crying during that difficult period. I was still employed part- time with Delta Airlines in Jacksonville, FL at that time and had been Retired from the Postal Service for a year, after 33 years of dedicated service.

Then the unfathomable happened. On December 8, 2010, after returning to work in Jacksonville, my manager at Delta informed me that they needed to take me home because Damien's only brother, my eldest son Shawn had been killed during the night. My heart shattered into a thousand pieces and God's Spirit again took me up and carried me through the excruciating ordeal of celebrating Shawn's life and burying him without being able to tell his brother Damien due to his fragile medical condition. In agony, I asked God, "why did you let Shawn die while I was out of town taking care of Damien? Why did you let him die before I got the chance to pray to you and plead for his life. His only answer to me was "It is well daughter. He is with me." Glory to God in the highest! Shawn left behind a 6 month old son, Elijah, three daughters, Andrea, Kiera, and Harmony and his eldest son, Shawn II. To be absent in the body is to be present with the Lord, but we still miss him dearly.

Meanwhile, Damien was still inundated with medicine and various procedures for sustaining his life. We had to convince the Nurses and Doctors to keep treating him because they didn't appear to think that he would make it out of his medical coma. He was still being fed from a tube in his stomach, had endured 18 days on a Respirator, pneumonia, a tracheotomy, having a hole drilled in his head to remove excess fluid, unable to feel his left side, double vision, and was unable to walk, talk or hold his head up. Again God's powerful spirit kept my mind from snapping and led me to focus on caring for what was left, my son Damien's long and miraculous recovery.

Let me fast forward to the present and testify of God's great power to heal. I give Glory to his name and know that because of His great mercy and grace toward us, the tube in Damien's stomach was removed and he is now eating solid food as he was before. Hallelujah!

He can feel and move his left side again although it is not YET strong enough to function as before. He takes Physical Therapy every week in God's plan to Rehab his body and regain his ability to walk. Hallelujah!

After almost 2 years, God restored his voice and he has taken Speech Therapy to learn how to talk all over again. Hallelujah!

His vision has come much closer together. Hallelujah!

His sound mind, Godly spirit, great character and personality have remained strong through it all. Hallelujah! He is off all medication except for an aspirin once or twice a week. Hallelujah!

We know that God is healing him daily and that more healing is coming because God is the God of more than enough! Hallelujah!

Although I had to resign from my part-time job in February 2011 to become Damien's full-time caretaker, God has supplied all of our needs and I've managed to keep my home despite the loss in income. Hallelujah!

After being Damien's only full-time caretaker for about a year, I am back singing and ministering Gospel Music with more love, passion and commitment than ever before. God is awesome! Hallelujah!

You see, we believe that God is able to do anything and we know that God never stopped loving us and has a greater plan for us in the building up of his Kingdom. God has kept us and given us the Peace that passes all understanding. We know that nothing shall be able to separate us from the love of God which is in Christ Jesus. We also know that the enemy meant it for bad but God is with us and is turning it around for our good. We believe that God will give us double for our trouble as he did for Job. We know that we don't have to fear because the Lord will prepare a table before us in the presence of our enemies. We also know that according to God's word, goodness and mercy is following us every day of our lives.

We thought it not robbery to share some of these prayers that we pray each morning with you. We continue to Trust and believe God for the Victory in this epic trial of our Faith. After becoming the prayer partner of my niece Jackie, a minister of the Gospel, God placed in my Spirit to publish these 31 Good Morning Prayers and share them and our testimony with others who are going through hard trials and tribulations in their life.

We are persuaded that it is Jehovah God, Jesus and the Holy

Spirit that are keeping our minds, fighting our battles and making a way of deliverance and victory for our lives each day. We know that God is not a respecter of persons, and that what he does for others he'll do for us. We believe that if we ask anything in Jesus name according to his will, it SHALL be done. We have faith in God! We trust God because we are living witnesses of his divine healing, grace and mercy!

So take it from us, Prayer changes things! We especially believe our heartfelt and powerful Morning Prayers, (referred to as "Prayer For Today or PFT") will jumpstart your spirit, prepare your mind to face the challenges of the day and remind you that you are covered by the redeeming blood of Jesus! We also accompany each prayer with a scripture from the King James Bible for each day, (referred to as the "Word For Today or WFT"), to feed your spirit and enhance your study of the word.

The Bible says that we have the Power of life and death in our tongues. Within these prayers we encourage you to Declare, Decree and Speak life in abundance over yourselves and your families every morning for a more excellent way of living. We believe that your best days are ahead of you, so begin your day with our God-inspired prayers to our Heavenly Father who loves us so much that he gave his only begotten son,

Jesus, to die on the Cross at Calvary, paying the price for our sins so that you and I might have a right to the tree of life and life more abundantly! We win! Hallelujah! Amen

God bless!

Ann Reynolds

Day 1

Good Morning (GM). The Word For Today (WFT) is found in Daniel 2:20-21. **The Prayer For Today (PFT)** is Heavenly Father we exalt You above the nations & ask that You forgive our trespasses as we forgive those who trespass against us. We thank You and we lay our burdens upon Your altar and leave them there knowing that all things work together for our good because we love You & are called according to Your purpose. We declare that the devil's grip on our lives cannot remain because what he meant for evil, God will turn around for our good. When we stand in Faith in Jesus name, all bondage is broken over our lives, our children, our marriage, our finances & our bodies in the mighty name of Jesus! We cry out to you for a great turnaround. You said in your word that You would give us beauty for ashes...joy for our pain...praise for our sadness...and dancing for our mourning. We love You God as we declare Victory and receive Your promises in Jesus name! **We win! Hallelujah! Amen**

<u>Scripture</u>

Daniel 2:20 Daniel answered and said, Blessed be the name of God for ever and ever: for wisdom and might are his:

21 And he changeth the times and the seasons: he removeth kings, and setteth up kings: he giveth wisdom unto the wise, and knowledge to them that know understanding:

<u>Day 2</u>

GM. The **WFT** is found in Matthew 8:7-8. The **PFT** is Heavenly Father we bless Your name on High. We bow before Your throne of grace and ask for Your blessings, healing, love & favor upon our lives & the lives of our families. Forgive us our trespasses as we forgive those who trespass against us. Thank you that we can depend on You for new mercies with the dawning of each new day. Thank You for your loving kindness & empowerment thru the Holy Spirit. Thank You that if we have faith the size of a grain of mustard seed, we can move the mountains in our lives out of our way. We Trust You with our lives and joyously receive an abundant & victorious life in Christ in the powerful name of Jesus.

We win! Hallelujah! Amen

Scripture

Matthew 8:7And Jesus saith unto him, I will come and heal him.

8 The centurion answered and said, Lord, I am not worthy that thou shouldest come under my roof: but speak the word only, and my servant shall be healed.

Good Morning Prayers

Day 3

GM. The **WFT** is found in 1 John 4:15-21. The **PFT** is Heavenly Father we acknowledge Your Holiness & Majesty today & Glorify You above the nations. We thank you for cleansing us from our sins and tossing them into the sea of forgetfulness. God we humble ourselves before You casting all our cares upon your altar with great expectancy of deliverance & divine protection for our families & this nation. We thank you that we can have confidence in You that if we ask anything according to Your will, You hear us. Because we know that You hear us, whatsoever we ask, we know that we have the petitions that we desire of You. So we declare that we are blessed when we go in & blessed when we go out! We declare that every good thing we put our hands to do is going to prosper & succeed! We declare Increase in our health, finances, relationships, jobs, faith, love and every other needful area of our lives & the lives of our families, friends & the body of Christ, in the matchless name of Jesus! **We Win! Hallelujah! Amen**

Scripture

1 John 4:15 Whosoever shall confess that Jesus is the Son of God, God dwelleth in him, and he in God.

16 And we have known and believed the love that God hath to us. God is love; and he that dwelleth in love dwelleth in God, and God in him.

17 Herein is our love made perfect, that we may have boldness in the day of judgment: because as he is, so are we in this world.

18 There is no fear in love; but perfect love casteth out fear: because fear hath torment. He that feareth is not made perfect in love.

19 We love him, because he first loved us.

20 If a man say, I love God, and hateth his brother, he is a liar: for he that loveth not his brother whom he hath seen, how can he love God whom he hath not seen?

21 And this commandment have we from him, That he who loveth God love his brother also.

Day 4

GM. The **WFT** is found in Proverbs 16:24. The **PFT** is Heavenly Father we bow humbly before Your Throne of Grace to Praise & Worship You in the beauty of Holiness today in Spirit & in Truth. Thank You for forgiving us for or debts as we forgive our debtors. We know that You are Omniscient knowing all things & Omnipotent having all Power to solve any problems in our lives. We marvel that Your Word says that You know what we are in need of before we ask, that You know the number of hairs on our heads & that You want us to Prosper & be in Good Health even as our Soul Prospers. Your Word says that we have the Power of Life & Death in our Tongues & that Pleasant Words are like a honeycomb, Sweetness to the Soul & Health to the bones. So by the Authority of the Blood of Jesus, we use the Power of your Word to Speak Abundant Life Overflowing, Healing, Encouragement, Peace, Prosperity, Kindness, Consideration of others, Generosity & Love over our Families as we Grow in Grace from day to day in the Matchless name of Jesus Christ our Lord! **We Win! Hallelujah! Amen**

<u>Scripture</u>

Proverbs 16:24 Pleasant words are as an honeycomb, sweet to the soul, and health to the bones.

<u>Day 5</u>

GM. The **WFT** is found in Philippians 4:4-8. The **PFT** is Heavenly Father we stretch our hands to you in Praise & Worship of Your Majesty & Omniscient Presence. We marvel at your grand creations & mighty acts and confess that there is none like You. We know because we searched all over, looked high & low and still couldn't find nobody Greater than You. So we bow before You and lay it all on Your alter in Thanksgiving & great expectation of your promises for our lives & the lives of our families now & forevermore. Because You said in your word that Goodness and Mercy shall follow us all the days of our lives, we shall walk in Victory and Love day by day in the mighty name of Jesus Christ our Lord & Savior! **We Win! Hallelujah! Amen**

Scripture

Philippians 4:4 Rejoice in the Lord always: and again I say, Rejoice.

5 Let your moderation be known unto all men. The Lord is at hand.

6 Be careful for nothing; but in everything by prayer and supplication with thanksgiving let your requests be made known unto God.

7 And the peace of God, which passeth all understanding, shall keep your hearts and minds through Christ Jesus.

8 Finally, brethren, whatsoever things are true, whatsoever things are honest, whatsoever things are just, whatsoever things are pure, whatsoever things are lovely, whatsoever things are of good report; if there be any virtue, and if there be any praise, think on these things.

Day 6

GM. The **WFT** is found in Romans 5:1-5. The **PFT** is Heavenly Father we humble ourselves before You today. We confess our sins and repent before you. Thank You for your forgiveness and thank You for supplying all of our needs according to Your riches in Glory thru Christ Jesus. Thank you for your riches of kindness, tolerance & patience toward us as we draw closer to You thru the trials & challenges of life. Help us to continue in brotherly love, rejoicing in hope & continuing to pray in season & out of season. Thank You that in you we have the power to pull down every stronghold in our lives & the lives of our children when we call on & trust in the great name of Jesus, our Lord, our strength & our redeemer. We praise You today & declare increase in our faith, increase in our health, increase in our finances, increase in our joy, increase in our love, and the peace that passeth all understanding in the matchless name of Jesus. We love you Lord & Heavenly Father! Increase! **We Win! Hallelujah! Amen**

Good Morning Prayers

<u>Scripture</u>

Romans 5:1 Therefore being justified by faith, we have peace with God through our Lord Jesus Christ:

2 By whom also we have access by faith into this grace wherein we stand, and rejoice in hope of the glory of God.

3 And not only so, but we glory in tribulations also: knowing that tribulation worketh patience;

4 And patience, experience; and hope:

5 And hope maketh not ashamed; because the love of God is shed abroad in our hearts by the Holy Ghost which is given unto us.

Day 7

GM. The **WFT** is found in 2 Timothy 1:6-7. The **PFT** is Heavenly Father we Love You, we Worship You, we Adore You, we hunger and thirst for your presence in our lives. Forgive us for anything that's not like You and cast it from us in the name of Jesus. Pour out Your mercy & grace upon us & our families. Restore us & redeem the time that the enemy has stolen from us and give us the Victory in all areas of our life. Thank You for loving us so much that we can come boldly to Your throne of Grace and cast all our cares upon you. Thank You that the battle is not ours, its the Lords. We receive Your Holy Spirit & limitless blessings today in the name of Jesus Christ our Redeemer and our Lord. **We Win! Hallelujah! Amen**

<u>Scripture</u>

6 2 Timothy 1:6 Wherefore I put thee in remembrance that thou stir up the gift of God, which is in thee by the putting on of my hands.

7 For God hath not given us the spirit of fear; but of power, and of love, and of a sound mind.

Day 8

GM. The **WFT** is found in Psalm 133:1 The **PFT** is Heavenly Father, Now unto the King Eternal, Immortal, Invisible, the only Wise God, be Honor & Glory Forever & Ever! We Worship You today in Spirit & in Truth because You've been good to us from the rising of the sun until the going down of the same. You're Worthy to be Praised & we lift our eyes & hands unto You because we know that all of our Help comes from You. We Love You & Thank You for forgiving us our trespasses as we forgive those who trespass against us. We thank You for the Families You have given to us to support & encourage one another as we journey thru life's seasons of sunshine & rain. We Thank You for Your Love & the Love of our Families that runs from heart to heart & according to Your Word, covers a multitude of sin. We Thank You for Your Holy Ghost Power & Favor! So by the Authority of the Blood of Jesus, we Declare that our Families are Covered, Healed, Saved, Delivered, Enabled, Prosperous, Blessed Going in and Blessed Coming out, in the Matchless name of Jesus! **We Win! Hallelujah! Amen**

<u>Scripture</u>

Psalm 133:1 Behold, how good and how pleasant it is for brethren to dwell together in unity!

Day 9

GM. The **WFT** is found in Romans 8:31-39. The **PFT** is Heavenly Father we Bless Your name on High & give You all the Glory & Honor for the great things that You do for us from day to day. We Love You & Thank You because You first Loved us & Delivered us from sin having dominion over us so that we might be called Your Sons & Daughters in Christ. We Thank You for forgiving us as we forgive others. We Praise & Worship You in Spirit & in Truth today and boldly receive Your Protection, Your Conquering Spirit, Your Giving Spirit, Your Divine Love, Your Divine Healing & the Peace that passes all understanding. So we Declare by the Authority of the Blood of Jesus that All of our families' Needs are met, that You shall do Exceedingly & Abundantly Above all that we can Ask or Think, Sound Minds, Healed Bodies, Healed Souls, Prosperity, More Faith, Favor, Increase & Joy Everlasting in the Mighty name of Jesus! We are Persuaded today that Nothing shall be able to Separate us from the Love of God which is in Christ Jesus our Lord! Increase! **We Win! Hallelujah! Amen**

<u>Scripture</u>

Romans 8:31 What shall we then say to these things? If God be for us, who can be against us?

32 He that spared not his own Son, but delivered him up for us all, how shall he not with him also freely give us all things?

33 Who shall lay any thing to the charge of God's elect? It is God that justifieth.

34 Who is he that condemneth? It is Christ that died, yea rather, that is risen again, who is even at the right hand of God, who also maketh intercession for us.

35 Who shall separate us from the love of Christ? shall tribulation, or distress, or persecution, or famine, or nakedness, or peril, or sword?

36 As it is written, For thy sake we are killed all the day long; we are accounted as sheep for the slaughter.

37 Nay, in all these things we are more than conquerors through him that loved us.

38 For I am persuaded, that neither death, nor life, nor angels, nor principalities, nor powers, nor things present, nor things to come,

39 Nor height, nor depth, nor any other creature, shall be able

to separate us from the love of God, which is in Christ Jesus our Lord.

Day 10

GM. The **WFT** is found in Colossians 3:14-17. The **PFT** is Holy & Heavenly Father we praise & honor you for Your mighty acts in our lives. We marvel how You have brought us & our families out of darkness into Your marvelous light. Forgive us our trespasses as we forgive those who trespass against us. Thank You for Your mercy & grace toward us and for Your unmerited favor which always gives us the victory in the name of Jesus. We love You & trust You with our lives today. Please continue to lead & guide us & we'll tell the story about how You brought us through storms & hard trials and stayed the hand of the enemy, turning every situation around for our good in the matchless name of Jesus. We receive your divine protection, power & love today. **We Win! Hallelujah! Amen**

<u>Scripture</u>

Colossians 3:14 And above all these things put on charity, which is the bond of perfectness.

15 And let the peace of God rule in your hearts, to the which also ye are called in one body; and be ye thankful.

16 Let the word of Christ dwell in you richly in all wisdom; teaching and admonishing one another in psalms and hymns and spiritual songs, singing with grace in your hearts to the Lord.

17 And whatsoever ye do in word or deed, do all in the name of the Lord Jesus, giving thanks to God and the Father by him.

Day 11

GM. The **WFT** is found in St Mark 11:22-26. The **PFT** is Heavenly Father we Praise and Worship You today for your Mercy, Grace & Favor in our lives & the lives of our families, friends & fellow Christians. Father forgive us for anything in us that is not like You & cast it out in the name of Jesus. Father You are Holy and we bless your omniscient presence. Thank you for your divine Guidance & Protection today. We praise You for food on our tables & clothes on our back. We thank you for the activity of our limbs and bless your Holy name. We declare & decree manifest breakthrough in our health, relationships & finances by the authority of the Blood of Jesus. Hallelujah! We boldly count it done In the name of Jesus! We trust & believe that we have received it by Your Spirit thru Christ Jesus. **We Win! Hallelujah! Amen**

<u>Scripture</u>

St Mark 11:22 And Jesus answering saith unto them, Have
faith in God.

23 For verily I say unto you, That whosoever shall say unto
this mountain, Be thou removed, and be thou cast into the
sea; and shall not doubt in his heart, but shall believe that
those things which he saith shall come to pass; he shall have
whatsoever he saith.

24 Therefore I say unto you, What things soever ye desire,
when ye pray, believe that ye receive them, and ye shall have
them.

25 And when ye stand praying, forgive, if ye have ought
against any: that your Father also which is in heaven may
forgive you your trespasses.

26 But if ye do not forgive, neither will your Father which is
in heaven forgive your trespasses.

Day 12

GM. The **WFT** is found in Hebrews 4:14:16. The **PFT** is Heavenly Father we Exalt Your Holy Name & Worship You in Spirit & Truth today. We come boldly to Your Throne of Grace in times of need seeking Your Mercy, Grace & Divine Help. We know that You are Omnipotent & that all things are Yours. We Thank You that You're God all by Yourself & that You will Open Doors for us that no man can shut. We thank You for forgiving us our trespasses as we forgive those who trespass against us. We thank you that You have delivered us from the Power of Darkness so that we can now walk in Your Marvelous Light. We Rejoice that You Restore us daily so that we may Encourage one another, be of one mind & live in Peace. We thank You that we are strengthened with Your Glorious Power which gives us all the Endurance & Patience we need to obtain the Victory for our lives & the lives of our families. So by the Authority of the Blood of Jesus, we Declare that we are Healed, Redeemed, Prosperous, Victorious & filled with the Joy of the Lord in Jesus name. **We Win! Hallelujah! Amen**

<u>Scripture</u>

14 Seeing then that we have a great high priest, that is passed into the heavens, Jesus the Son of God, let us hold fast our profession.

15 For we have not an high priest which cannot be touched with the feeling of our infirmities; but was in all points tempted like as we are, yet without sin.

16 Let us therefore come boldly unto the throne of grace, that we may obtain mercy, and find grace to help in time of need.

<u>Day 13</u>

GM. The **WFT** is found in Ephesians 1:10-18. The **PFT** is thank You Heavenly Father for this opportunity to come before Your throne of Grace once more to worship You in Spirit & in Truth. We are in awe of Your faithful & longsuffering Love for us even when we have been unfaithful to You. We marvel at how You keep forgiving us over & over again and how You keep picking us up, cleaning us off and giving us another chance to live our lives with Your purpose in mind. We pray today that You reveal to us again, with that still soft voice, what it is You have purposed for us to do in our lives & the lives of others for the sake of Your kingdom in this present world. We find Strength & the Confidence to firmly stand our ground against the attacks of the enemy & after we've done all, to stand... and see the Salvation of the Lord! We declare that when the enemy comes in, like a flood God will set up a standard against them. We declare God's sudden breakthrough in our family's health, our relationships, finances & ministries today in the name of Jesus! **We Win! Hallelujah! Amen**

Scripture

Ephesians 1:10 That in the dispensation of the fulness of times he might gather together in one all things in Christ, both which are in heaven, and which are on earth; even in him:

11 In whom also we have obtained an inheritance, being predestinated according to the purpose of him who worketh all things after the counsel of his own will:

12 That we should be to the praise of his glory, who first trusted in Christ.

13 In whom ye also trusted, after that ye heard the word of truth, the gospel of your salvation: in whom also after that ye believed, ye were sealed with that holy Spirit of promise,

14 Which is the earnest of our inheritance until the redemption of the purchased possession, unto the praise of his glory.

15 Wherefore I also, after I heard of your faith in the Lord Jesus, and love unto all the saints,

16 Cease not to give thanks for you, making mention of you in my prayers;

17 That the God of our Lord Jesus Christ, the Father of glory, may give unto you the spirit of wisdom and revelation in the

knowledge of him:

18 The eyes of your understanding being enlightened; that ye may know what is the hope of his calling, and what the riches of the glory of his inheritance in the saints

Day 14

GM. The **WFT** is found in Luke 10:19 & Luke 11:9. The **PFT** is Heavenly Father You are our Great Jehovah, Abba Father, Ancient of Days, The Great I AM & we worship & praise Your Holy name. Father we thank You for the authority You've given us to bind Satan's power over our lives & the lives of our loved ones. We declare that by the authority of the Blood of Jesus, we command that the spirit of sickness, lack, depression, self-condemnation, doubt, defeat, bondage & fear bow down to the Spirit of God in us and flee back to the pit of hell from whence it came, in the name of Jesus! We release & declare the spirit of good health, abundance, joy, self-confidence, a sound mind, victory, freedom & courage in Jesus name! We declare that no weapon formed against us will be able to prosper and that all things are working together for our good because we love You God & know that we are called according to your purpose! We thank you in advance for deliverance, for empowerment & for enriching our lives daily & we give You the highest Praise. **We Win! Hallelujah! Amen**

Good Morning Prayers

Scripture

Luke 10:19 Behold, I give unto you power to tread on serpents and scorpions, and over all the power of the enemy: and nothing shall by any means hurt you.
Luke 11:9 And I say unto you, Ask, and it shall be given you; seek, and ye shall find; knock, and it shall be opened unto you.

Day 15

GM. The **WFT** is found in Isaiah 43:1-3. The **PFT** is Heavenly Father we acknowledge You today in Praise & Worship of Your Omniscient Presence. We worship You because You are Alpha & Omega. You know the beginning & the end of our lives and we praise You for the guidance of Your Holy Spirit. We thank You that when we confess our sins, You are faithful & just to forgive us and to cleanse us from all unrighteousness. We thank You that NOTHING shall be able to separate us from the Love of God which is in Christ Jesus. Therefore we love You back Holy God. We study to show ourselves approved unto You, needing not to be ashamed, but rightly dividing the word of truth. We thank You that You have not given us a Spirit of Fear, but of Power, & of Love, & of a Sound Mind. Today we boldly declare Salvation, Healing, Peace, Prosperity, Love, Faith, Righteousness, Patience, Sanctification, Holiness, Joy and an unfailing Faith in You for us & our families, in the matchless name of Jesus Christ, our Lord and Savior! **We Win! Hallelujah! Amen**

Scripture

Isaiah 43:1 But now thus saith the Lord that created thee, O Jacob, and he that formed thee, O Israel, Fear not: for I have redeemed thee, I have called thee by thy name; thou art mine.
2 When thou passest through the waters, I will be with thee; and through the rivers, they shall not overflow thee: when thou walkest through the fire, thou shalt not be burned; neither shall the flame kindle upon thee.
3 For I am the Lord thy God, the Holy One of Israel, thy Saviour: I gave Egypt for thy ransom, Ethiopia and Seba for thee.

Day 16

GM. The **WFT** is found in Lamentations 3:21-26. The **PFT** is Heavenly Father we praise & worship You today because You are so faithful to us that, according to Your Word, Your Mercies are new EVERY morning. Glory to Your name because You are the God that Forgives our sins and Heals us. Thank You for waking us up this morning, putting a roof over our heads and putting food on our table. Thank You that our children & grandchildren have also been deemed heirs to Your Promises thru Christ Jesus our Lord & Savior. So by the authority of the blood of Jesus we break every chain of bondage, rebellion, and disobedience. Through Prayer we loose God's liberty, obedience and a sound mind upon their lives. We decree that they are covered by the blood of Jesus to become over comers in every area of their lives. We also declare that God shall supply all of our needs according to his riches in Glory thru Christ Jesus. We decree divine Protection, Peace, Love, Prosperity, Healing, Faith, Grace & Victory upon our lives today in the mighty name of Jesus! **We Win! Hallelujah! Amen**

<u>Scripture</u>

Lamentations 3:21 This I recall to my mind, therefore have I hope.

22 It is of the Lᴏʀᴅ's mercies that we are not consumed, because his compassions fail not.

23 They are new every morning: great is thy faithfulness.

24 The Lᴏʀᴅ is my portion, saith my soul; therefore will I hope in him.

25 The Lᴏʀᴅ is good unto them that wait for him, to the soul that seeketh him.

26 It is good that a man should both hope and quietly wait for the salvation of the Lᴏʀᴅ.

Day 17

GM. The **WFT** is found in Galatians 6:9. The **PFT** is Heavenly Father, we humble ourselves at Your throne of Grace today to Worship You in Spirit & in Truth. We thank You for forgiving us our debts as we forgive our debtors. We humbly acknowledge that You are all-knowing & all-powerful & that we can't do anything without You breathing Your Breath of Life into us morning by morning. We realize that If we count our blessings and name them one by one, we wouldn't be able to count them all. We thank You that you've been so good to us & our families thru the years. We thank You for continuing to save & deliver us when our own misguided decisions lead us into a hard place. Thank You God that Your unchanging hand is ever reaching out to us and that the battle is not ours, it's the Lord's. Finally God, today we will do as Your word tells us and be Strong in the Lord & in the Power of his Might. We declare Your divine Healing, Prosperity, Joy, Peace, Love, Wisdom, Faith, Patience & Power over our families in the Mighty name of Jesus! We love You God! **We Win! Hallelujah! Amen**

Scripture

Galatians 6:9 And let us not be weary in well doing: for in due season we shall reap, if we faint not

Good Morning Prayers

Day 18

GM. The **WFT** is found in John 3:16-18. The **PFT** is Heavenly Father we praise, honor & worship You & give You the Glory for keeping us from day to day. Thank You for forgiving us our trespasses as we forgive those who trespass against us. We lift Your name on High because You are Worthy. We thank You for being our Jehovah Jirah, Our Provider, Jehovah Rappha, Our Healer, Jehovah Shamma, You are with us, Jehovah Nissi, You fight our battles, Jehovah Shalom, You are our Peace and Jehovah Mechidishem, You are our Sanctifier! We thank You that nothing can separate us from Your Love which is in Christ Jesus. Thank You that You love us so much that You gave Your only begotten son, so that whosoever believes in You should not perish but have Everlasting Life and Life more abundantly. So today we declare that the plans of the enemy are broken & canceled by the authority of the blood of Jesus! Instead we declare Divine INCREASE in Health, Love, Wisdom, Good Works, Faith, Finances, Peace & Joy for our families in the Mighty name of Jesus! Hallelujah! Amen **We Win! Hallelujah! Amen**

Scripture

John 3:16 For God so loved the world, that he gave his only begotten Son, that whosoever believeth in him should not perish, but have everlasting life.

17 For God sent not his Son into the world to condemn the world; but that the world through him might be saved.

18 He that believeth on him is not condemned: but he that believeth not is condemned already, because he hath not believed in the name of the only begotten Son of God.

Day 19

GM. The **WFT** is found in Proverbs 11:2. The **PFT** is Heavenly Father we humble ourselves before You this day that You have made and we will Rejoice and be glad in it. We thank You for Your Grace & Mercy toward us in that You forgive us our trespasses as we forgive those who trespass against us. We Praise You for Your Mighty Acts in our lives & Worship Your Omniscient Presence in the lives of our families. We know that in Your presence there is Peace, Love, Joy, Healing, Strength, Saving Grace, Deliverance, Divine Guidance of the Holy Spirit and the Power to Prosper in everything we put our hands to do! We thank You God that your Word says that "If ye Abide in me and my Words Abide in you, ye shall ask what ye will and it shall be done unto You." Help us to study Your Word & keep it in our hearts so that we won't sin against You nor pray amiss. God You said that You would withhold NO GOOD thing from those who walk upright before You. Because of Your Grace we receive Your Promises and are counted as the Righteousness of You by the shed blood of Jesus! **We Win! Hallelujah! Amen**

Scripture

Proverbs 11:2 When pride cometh, then cometh shame: but with the lowly is wisdom.

Day 20

GM. The **WFT** for today is found in 1 Corinthians 13:4-8 and 13-13. The **PFT** is Heavenly Father You are Holy and worthy to be Praised & Worshiped in Spirit & in Truth. You are Good, Compassionate & Merciful unto us & our offspring even when we make bad decisions in our lives. You are always there to deliver us from every mistake or stumbling block that the enemy places in our path. You continually forgive us for our debts as we forgive our debtors & for that we thank You. We love You God because You first loved us. Father You have brought us from a mighty long way & we don't believe You brought us this far to leave us. We Rejoice thru hard times, trials & tribulations because we know that You will never leave us nor forsake us but will take us all the way thru the storms of life & triumphantly place our feet on higher ground. So we continue to study your Word, pray, & Faithfully Declare that our bodies are Healed & Strong, that Love, Joy and Prosperity will overtake us today by the Authority of the Blood of Jesus! Thank You God! **We Win! Hallelujah! Amen**

<u>Scripture</u>

1 Corinthians 13:4 Charity suffereth long, and is kind; charity envieth not; charity vaunteth not itself, is not puffed up;

5. Doth not behave itself unseemly, seeketh not her own, is not easily provoked, thinketh no evil;

6. Rejoiceth not in iniquity, but rejoiceth in the truth;

7. Beareth all things, believeth all things, hopeth all things, endureth all things.

8. Charity never faileth 1 Corinthians 13:13 And now abideth faith, hope, charity,

these three; but the greatest of these is charity.

Day 21

GM. The **WFT** is found in Isaiah 41:10 & 13. The **PFT** is Heavenly Father we Love & Adore You for Your Faithfulness to us even when we are not Faithful to You. We marvel that You have such a Great Love for us so we Praise & Worship You in Spirit & in Truth. We thank You for blotting out our transgressions & tossing our sins into the sea of forgetfulness. Thank You for giving us a Clean Heart & renewing a right Spirit within us. Thank You that Your Mercies are New every day. Thank You for restoring our Souls & leading us in the path of Righteousness. So by the Authority of the Blood of Jesus, we come against the plans of the enemy today knowing that our families are Covered by the Redeeming Blood of Jesus! We declare Your word which says that You are the God who gives us the Power to get Wealth; the God who Heals us from all our Diseases; the God who Delivers us from all our Troubles; the God who is Mighty in Battle; the God who is Love and the God of Peace! We receive Your Blessings this day & claim the Victory in the name of Jesus! **We Win! Hallelujah! Amen**

Scripture

Isaiah 41:10 Fear thou not; for I am with thee; be not dismayed; for I am thy God; I will strengthen thee; yea, I will help thee; yea, I will uphold thee with the right hand of my righteousness.

Isaiah 41:13 For I the Lord thy God will hold thy right hand, saying unto thee, Fear not; I will help thee.

Day 22

GM. The **WFT** for today is found in Psalms 1:1-3. The **PFT** is Heavenly Father we thank You for letting us see the dawn of a new day. We know that because of Your Mercy & Your Love for us, we & our families are Forgiven, Redeemed, & set Free to have life and life more abundantly. So we pay it forward & forgive those who trespass against us. Because of Your Unmerited Favor, we know that we are a Royal Priesthood & Children of the Most High God ! We Love & Adore You Father! You are Wonderful, Glorious, Holy & Righteous, Victorious, Conqueror, Triumphant & Mighty, Healer, Deliverer, Shield & Defense, Strong Tower, our Best Friend, Omnipotent, Omnipresent, Succor Redeemer, Alpha, Omega, and Lord of Everything! Who wouldn't serve a God like You! We lift Your name on High Jehovah God & receive Your Holy anointing in our lives as we declare Your Overcoming Power, Healing, Salvation, Deliverance, Joy, Love, Prosperity & Peace. May it Rest, Rule & Abide in us as we walk in Victory & Favor thru this life in the name of Jesus Christ our Lord! **We Win! Hallelujah! Amen**

<u>Scripture</u>

Psalms 1:1 Blessed is the man that walketh not in the counsel of the ungodly, nor standeth in the way of sinners, nor sitteth in the seat of the scornful.

2 But his delight is in the law of the Lord; and in his law doth he meditate day and night.

3 And he shall be like a tree planted by the rivers of water, that bringeth forth his fruit in his season; his leaf also shall not wither; and whatsoever he doeth shall prosper.

<u>Day 23</u>

GM. The **WFT** is found in Psalm 91:9-12. The **PFT** is Heavenly Father we humble ourselves before Your Throne today & Praise & Worship You in Spirit & in Truth. We are so Grateful that we are Your Children & that Your Word promises that You will never leave us nor forsake us. We thank You for forgiving us our trespasses as we forgive those who trespass against us. We thank you that we are Saved by Your Grace & not by works. We thank you that Everything is working together for our good because we love You and are called according to Your purpose. We thank You that You are supplying all our needs according to Your riches in Glory by Christ Jesus. We thank You that no weapon formed against us shall be able to prosper & that when we resist the devil, he Must Flee from us. So by the authority of the Blood of Jesus, we bind & cast out the Spirit of Fear, Lack, Sickness and Defeat. We release the Spirit of Encouragement, Wealth, Good Health, and Victory over us & our families as we fight the good fight of Faith in the name of Jesus Christ! **We Win! Hallelujah! Amen**

Scripture

Psalm 91:9 Because thou hast made the Lord, which is my refuge, even the most High, thy habitation;

10 There shall no evil befall thee, neither shall any plague come nigh thy dwelling.

11 For he shall give his angels charge over thee, to keep thee in all thy ways.

12 They shall bear thee up in their hands, lest thou dash thy foot against a stone.

Day 24

GM. The **WFT** is found in Proverb 3:5-6. The **PFT** is Heavenly Father we Love You, we Praise You, we Honor You, we Trust You & we Worship You in Spirit & in Truth today for who You are. You are such a Great & Loving God & Father that we can Trust You while we sleep, we can Trust You as we go about our activities each day, we can Trust You on our jobs, we can Trust You as we travel in our cars or fly on planes. You wake us up with Your breath of life from day to day & fill us with Your Loving & Overcoming Spirit so that we can handle every situation throughout the constantly changing seasons of our lives. We thank you that thru it all, Your great Love for us never changes. You continue to Guide, Heal, Comfort, Rescue & Deliver us from every situation. You dust us off, tend to our heartfelt wounds, block the plans of the enemy, encourage us, turn it around for our Good and do exceedingly and abundantly above all that we can ask or think. So we thank You & boldly Declare that the chains are Broken & that we have the Victory in Jesus name! **We Win! Hallelujah! Amen**

Scripture

Proverb 3:5 Trust in the Lord with all thine heart; and lean not unto thine own understanding.

6 In all thy ways acknowledge him, and he shall direct thy paths

Day 25

GM. The **WFT** is found in 1 Corinthians 15:57-58. The **PFT** is Heavenly Father we Love & Adore You today because You loved us when we were unlovable. We thank You for reaching down in the midst of our mess, picking us up and placing our feet on Your solid rock to stay. Thank You for forgiving us our trespasses as we forgive those who trespass against us. Thank You for loving us so much that you gave Your only begotten son Jesus so that we might be set free to have Life more abundantly. We thank You that because Jesus rose with all Power, Your word says that Greater works will we do when we receive the Power of Your Word by Faith. We marvel that because Christ Jesus has Overcome the World for us we also are Over comers in this Life. The plans of the enemy are Defeated & he has no Authority over us. So by the Authority of the Blood of Jesus we Declare Healing for our bodies & souls, Breakthrough in our Finances, Beauty for ashes, Wisdom, Courage, Strength, Peace, Love & the Favor of God for our families today in the name of Jesus! **We Win! Hallelujah! Amen**

<u>Scripture</u>

1 Corinthians 15:57 But thanks be to God, which giveth us the victory through our Lord Jesus Christ.

58 Therefore, my beloved brethren, be ye steadfast, unmoveable, always abounding in the work of the Lord, forasmuch as ye know that your labour is not in vain in the Lord.

Day 26

GM. The **WFT** is found in Isaiah 40:29-31. The **PFT** is Heavenly Father we Bless Your name on High because You are Holy & Righteous & Merciful unto us. We Praise & Worship You in Spirit & in Truth today because You are Worthy of Honor & Glory. We thank You for forgiving us our debts as we forgive our debtors. We thank You that because Your Holy Spirit in us is Mighty, we are Saved, Healed, Set Free & Delivered. When we call on that Great name of Jesus. Help us to walk worthy of our calling by being a good example of a Believer, in Word, in Conversation, in Love, in Spirit and in Faith. Help us to show our children & our grandchildren how to walk in Your ways so that they may reap the benefits of Joy, Richness, Love, Health & Strength as a child of the King. Help us to Encourage them as we Encourage ourselves in the Lord in every situation. We Trust You God! So by the Authority of the Blood of Jesus we Declare that our families are Blessed, Healed, Saved, Delivered, & Prosperous in the Mighty name of Jesus! **We Win! Hallelujah! Amen**

<u>Scripture</u>

Isaiah 40:29 He giveth power to the faint; and to them that have no might he increaseth strength.

30 Even the youths shall faint and be weary, and the young men shall utterly fall:

31 But they that wait upon the Lord shall renew their strength; they shall mount up with wings as eagles; they shall run, and not be weary; and they shall walk, and not faint.

<u>Day 27</u>

GM. The **WFT** is found in Peter 2:9-10. The **PFT** is Heavenly Father we Bless Your name & give You the Glory & Honor that You deserve because You are Worthy. We Praise You in the Sanctuary and in our homes because our Faith & Trust is in You & the finished work of Jesus Christ our Lord who thought it not robbery to give his life for us, paying the price for our sins so that we can be set free and have life more abundantly. We thank You for forgiving us as we forgive others. We thank You that we are counted as the Righteousness of God and we marvel that you have placed Your Holy Spirit down on the inside of us to lead & guide us into all knowledge & Truth. We Pray for Your Favor upon our families today and boldly Declare Your Divine Love, Health, Sound Mind, Overcoming Spirit, Joy, Peace & Saving Grace over every situation in the Powerful name of Jesus! Your word says that we can cast down wrong thoughts & renew them because as we think, so are we. So today we Declare that we are Blessed & Highly Favored & that we are Victors, not Victims! **We Win! Hallelujah! Amen**

Scripture

Peter 2:9 But ye are a chosen generation, a royal priesthood, a holy nation, a peculiar people; that ye should shew forth the praises of him who hath called you out of darkness into his marvelous light;

10 Which in time past were not a people, but are now the people of God: which had not obtained mercy, but now have obtained mercy.

Day 28

GM. The **WFT** is found in Titus 2:1-8. The **PFT** is Heavenly Father we Humble ourselves before You today & acknowledge Your Omnipotence in our lives. Your word says that You are God & that from the rising of the sun & the going down of the same, there is None like You. We give You Glory & Worship You in Spirit & in Truth today seeking Your Blessings, Guidance, Miracles and Mercies that are new for us everyday. Thank You for forgiving us our debts as we forgive our debtors. We receive Your Word which says be careful for nothing; but in everything by Prayer & Supplication with Thanksgiving, let your requests be made known unto God. Then the Peace of God which passeth all understanding shall keep our hearts & minds through Christ Jesus. So we do not Fear, but we Believe & Meditate on whatsoever things are true, whatsoever things are honest, whatsoever things are Pure, whatsoever things are lovely, whatsoever things are of Good Report, Virtue & Praise. In the name of Jesus we boldly Declare that we are Healed, that our Needs are met and that **We Win! Hallelujah! Amen**

Scripture

Titus 2:1 But speak thou the things which become sound doctrine:

2 That the aged men be sober, grave, temperate, sound in faith, in charity, in patience.

3 The aged women likewise, that they be in behavior as becometh holiness, not false accusers, not given to much wine, teachers of good things;

4 That they may teach the young women to be sober, to love their husbands, to love their children,

5 To be discreet, chaste, keepers at home, good, obedient to their own husbands, that the word of God be not blasphemed.

6 Young men likewise exhort to be sober minded.

7 In all things shewing thyself a pattern of good works: in doctrine shewing uncorruptness, gravity, sincerity,

8 Sound speech, that cannot be condemned; that he that is of the contrary part may be ashamed, having no evil thing to say of you.

Day 29

GM. The **WFT** is found in Psalm 133:1 The **PFT** is Heavenly Father, Now unto the King Eternal, Immortal, Invisible, the only Wise God, be Honor & Glory Forever & Ever! We Worship You today in Spirit and in Truth because You've been good to us from the rising of the sun until the going down of the same. You're Worthy to be Praised and we lift our eyes & hands unto You because we know that all of our Help comes from You. We Love You and Thank You for forgiving us our trespasses as we forgive those who trespass against us. We thank You for the Families You have given to us to support and encourage one another as we journey thru life's seasons of sunshine & rain. We Thank You for Your Love & the Love of our Families that runs from heart to heart & according to Your Word, covers a multitude of sin. We Thank You for Your Holy Ghost Power & Favor! So by the Authority of the Blood of Jesus, we Declare that our Families are Covered, Healed, Saved, Delivered, Enabled, Prosperous, Blessed Going in and Blessed Coming out, in the Matchless name of Jesus! **We Win! Hallelujah! Amen**

Scripture

Psalm 133:1 Behold, how good and how pleasant it is for brethren to dwell together in unity!

Day 30

GM. The **WFT** is found in Romans 8:31-39. The **PFT** is Heavenly Father we Bless Your name on High & give You all the Glory & Honor for the great things that You do for us from day to day. We Love You & Thank You because You first Loved us & Delivered us from sin having dominion over us so that we might be called Your Sons & Daughters in Christ. We Thank You for forgiving us as we forgive others. We Praise & Worship You in Spirit & in Truth today and boldly receive Your Protection, Your Conquering Spirit, Your Giving Spirit, Your Divine Love, Your Divine Healing & the Peace that passes all understanding. So we Declare by the Authority of the Blood of Jesus that All of our families' Needs are met, that You shall do Exceedingly & Abundantly Above all that we can Ask or Think, Sound Minds, Healed Bodies, Healed Souls, Prosperity, More Faith, Favor, Increase & Joy Everlasting in the Mighty name of Jesus! We are Persuaded today that Nothing shall be able to Separate us from the Love of God which is in Christ Jesus our Lord! Increase! **We Win! Hallelujah! Amen**

<u>Scripture</u>

Romans 8:31 What shall we then say to these things? If God be for us, who can be against us?

32 He that spared not his own Son, but delivered him up for us all, how shall he not with him also freely give us all things?

33 Who shall lay any thing to the charge of God's elect? It is God that justifieth.

34 Who is he that condemneth? It is Christ that died, yea rather, that is risen again, who is even at the right hand of God, who also maketh intercession for us.

35 Who shall separate us from the love of Christ? shall tribulation, or distress, or persecution, or famine, or nakedness, or peril, or sword?

36 As it is written, For thy sake we are killed all the day long; we are accounted as sheep for the slaughter.

37 Nay, in all these things we are more than conquerors through him that loved us.

38 For I am persuaded, that neither death, nor life, nor angels, nor principalities, nor powers, nor things present, nor things to come,

39 Nor height, nor depth, nor any other creature, shall be able

to separate us from the love of God, which is in Christ Jesus our Lord.

Day 31

GM. The **WFT** is found in Psalm 91:1-7. The **PFT** is Heavenly Father, Great is thy Faithfulness toward us! We shout Glory & Honor unto Your Holy & Almighty name Jehovah in all the earth! You are Jehovah Jirah, our Provider; Jehovah Rappha, our Healer; & Jehovah Shalom, our Peace. We thank You for Your Divine Covering & Protection & Worship You in Spirit & Truth today. We Thank You for forgiving us as we forgive others & we come Boldly to Your Throne of Grace laying our Burdens down upon Your Altar. For we know that You are an On-time God who calls those things that be not as though they were & they Are. We know You to be the God that spoke the World into existence & who Raised our Lord & Savior Jesus Christ from the Dead with All Power! The God who instructed us in Your Word to do the same by placing the Power of Life & Death in Our Tongues. So by Faith & the Authority of the Blood of Jesus we open our mouths today & Speak Life to our Health, Life to our Relationships, Life to our Finances and Life to our Joy in the Mighty name of Jesus! **We Win! Hallelujah! Amen**

Scripture

Psalm 91:1 He that dwelleth in the secret place of the most High shall abide under the shadow of the Almighty.

2 I will say of the Lord, He is my refuge and my fortress: my God; in him will I trust.

3 Surely he shall deliver thee from the snare of the fowler, and from the noisome pestilence.

4 He shall cover thee with his feathers, and under his wings shalt thou trust: his truth shall be thy shield and buckler.

5 Thou shalt not be afraid for the terror by night; nor for the arrow that flieth by day;

6 Nor for the pestilence that walketh in darkness; nor for the destruction that wasteth at noonday.

7 A thousand shall fall at thy side, and ten thousand at thy right hand; but it shall not come nigh thee.

FOREWORD

It has been a privilege & an honor to share my "Good Morning" prayers to our Heavenly Father with you in the precious name of Jesus. We hope and pray that your spirits have been quickened and filled with the Love, Peace and Power of God to walk as Over comers in this world by putting your trust, faith and confidence in Him morning by morning. We pray that your outlook on your life has dramatically changed for the better or has been refreshed anew with great joy and expectation of a victorious future for you and your families. Thank you for receiving them in the spirit of love & fellowship in Christ Jesus. Our God is Awesome!

We also hope that you will read a prayer each morning before you begin your day and tell others about this precious book of Good Morning prayers divinely given to me by God during my season of trauma and struggle. These prayers help us to endure this season and still have joy while God continues to prosper and heal us. This too shall pass and we are persuaded that in Christ, our best days are still ahead of us!

I love you all with the love of the Lord and encourage you to continue to have Faith, Strength & Joy in the Holy Ghost! Weeping endures for a night, but Joy comes in the morning. Declare & Speak Life daily and do as the Word instructs us in Proverbs 3:5-6; " Trust in the Lord with all your heart, lean not to your own understanding; in all your ways acknowledge Him & He shall Direct your Paths!"

We Win! Hallelujah! Amen

Ann Reynolds

* 9 7 8 0 6 1 5 9 7 0 1 9 6 *